SHEILA E.

A Real-Life Reader Biography

Christine Granados

Mitchell Lane Publishers, Inc.
P.O. Box 200 • Childs, Maryland 21916

First Printing
Real-Life Reader Biographies

Selena	Robert Rodriguez	Mariah Carey	Rafael Palmeiro
Tommy Nuñez	Trent Dimas	Cristina Saralegui	Andres Galarraga
Oscar De La Hoya	Gloria Estefan	Jimmy Smits	Mary Joe Fernandez
Cesar Chavez	Chuck Norris	Sinbad	Paula Abdul
Vanessa Williams	Celine Dion	Mia Hamm	Sammy Sosa
Brandy	Michelle Kwan	Rosie O'Donnell	Shania Twain
Garth Brooks	Jeff Gordon	Mark McGwire	Salma Hayek
Sheila E.	Hollywood Hogan	Ricky Martin	Britney Spears
Arnold Schwarzenegger			

Library of Congress Cataloging-in-Publication Data
Granados, Christine, 1969-
      Sheila E./Christine Granados.
         p. cm. — (A real-life reader biography)
      Includes index.
      Summary: Describes the life of Sheila E., singer and percussionist, from growing up in Oakland, to playing with various bands, to her success as the first female band director on late-night TV.
      ISBN 1-58415-019-X
      1. E., Sheila (Escovedo), 1959- Juvenile literature. 2. Singers —United States Biography Juvenile literature. 3. Percussionists—United States Biography Juvenile literature. [1. E., Sheila (Escovedo), 1959- . 2. Musicians. 3. Women Biography.] I. Title. II. Series.
ML3930.E2G73 1999
781.64'092—dc21
[B]
                                          99-25254
                                             CIP

ABOUT THE AUTHOR: Christine Granados has been a writer and editor for many years. She was recently the editor of *Moderna* magazine and has been a newspaper reporter for *The El Paso Times, Austin American-Statesman,* and *Long Beach Press-Telegram.* She is a contributing author to the **Contemporary American Success Stories** series (Mitchell Lane), authored Rosie O'Donnell (Mitchell Lane) and has published numerous magazine feature stories.

PHOTO CREDITS: cover: Globe Photos; p. 4, 18 courtesy Sheila E.; p. 7 Ralph Dominguez/ Globe Photos; p. 16 Globe Photos; p. 20 Sunny Bak/Shooting Star; p. 23, 25 Globe Photos; p. 31 AP PhotoReview Journal/Craig L. Moran.

ACKNOWLEDGMENTS: The following story has been written based on the author's personal interviews with Sheila E. and her family in May 1998 and again in February 1999. It has been approved for print by Sheila E. To the best of our knowledge, this represents a true story.

Table of Contents

Sheila E.

4

Chapter 1
Standing Up
for Herself

Imagine a fifteen-year-old girl telling a man more than twice her age that she was old enough and talented enough to play the drums and congas in his band. Think about the guts it takes to stand up for yourself and believe in yourself. It can be even harder to do when that man is your father. Sheila E. did it. She told her father, Pete Escovedo, a world-famous percussion player, that she could play in his band. Pete was the leader of a band called Azteca that played music in the 1970s. She told him that she could fill in for his regular percussionist, who was sick.

At the age of fifteen, Sheila told her father she wanted to play with his band.

What Pete saw was a young, skinny, curly-haired girl whose only experience on drums was playing for a band made up of her high school friends. The thirty-eight-year-old father of four didn't believe that his daughter could handle playing in front of a lot of people. Azteca toured all over the world and played in front of governors, mayors, and audiences that could fill a football stadium. In fact, he wasn't even sure that she knew how to play the instrument or could play the music.

"Pops, I can play this music. I know the songs," Sheila insisted.

With the help of her mother and the soft spot her father held for her, Sheila got a chance to audition for Azteca. "I told Pete, 'Honey, why don't you try Sheila?'" Juanita Escovedo, Sheila's mother, remembered. "But he didn't want to hear it. He said, 'For one thing the girl is fifteen years old, and the band is going to Bogata, Colombia and there is no way I'm going to take my daughter on the road. She's just not going to be good enough.' That's when I said, 'Pete, just try her!' He really didn't have a choice."

So during the next rehearsal at the Escovedo house, Sheila played for her father and his band. "He was really, really amazed and shocked," Sheila recalled with a laugh. "I didn't know, and he didn't know, how much I had learned by just being in the house and absorbing the music everyday, by just having the band around playing, rehearsing, and his practicing to records."

Sheila with Lionel Ritchie

Sheila has been amazing and shocking people ever since. She has toured with many musicians such as the artist then known as Prince, Plácido Domingo, Gloria Estefan, Lionel Richie, Herbie Hancock, and Diana Ross, and was musical director and band leader of the Earvin "Magic" Johnson show, *The Magic Hour*, which appeared on the Fox network for a short time.

Chapter 2
Growing Up Poor

Sheila Cecilia Escovedo was born December 12, 1957 in Oakland, California to Juanita Gardere and Pete Escovedo. She was the first of four children.

Juanita and Pete met in the 1950s. "I first noticed Pete in junior high. I thought he was so cute," Juanita said. "He was always dressed so nice with his suede shoes and jacket and tie. We started talking and walking home from school together. He lived in West Oakland and I lived in North Oakland. It was about 40 minutes away."

Pete's memory is a little different. "I was going downtown and hanging out. I saw Juanita walking by to a place called Walgreens. It was a soda fountain [an ice cream parlor]. My friends went to her school. It was a better school. I went to school in the ghetto. My friend told me I had to come over to this family's house [where Juanita lived]. I went over there and the rest, as they say, is history."

They were married in October 1956 and Sheila was born a year later. Juanita's parents, Nicolas Gardere and Marie Pelletier, from New Orleans, Louisiana, didn't approve of their daughter's marriage to a musician, but Juanita knew the two would make a wonderful pair.

At the time Pete played percussion on weekends, while Juanita was part of the Teamsters Union and worked in ice cream and cheese factories. It was conveyor belt work. "My job helped Pete keep playing, which I had no problem with," Juanita said. "I wanted to work and he wanted to play music. He basically raised the kids."

Pete said the family struggled along. "Juanita knew music was what I wanted to do. I knew how hard it was going to be. I pumped gas and worked

Her father, Pete, played in a band, and her mother, Juanita worked in ice cream and cheese factories.

in a cannery. I was a house mother. At night when I had a gig [a job playing music], I would take Sheila with me. She would watch me play. Some of the owners of the bars would say, 'Hey you can't bring a kid in here.' I said, 'What do you expect me to do? I can't come to work unless I bring her.' I took her everywhere."

Growing up with musicians coming in and out of her house, and listening to Tito Puente, Tito Rodriguez, and Dizzy Gillespie playing in her living room, it's no surprise that Sheila picked up the congas at an early age. As a three-year-old, Sheila would stand in front of the wooden and cow-skinned three-foot-high drums when she was just two feet tall. Her father sat behind the instrument, and with her hands high above her head, unable to see what she was mimicking, Sheila repeated her father's quick drumbeats. Because of this early training, to this day Sheila plays the congas backwards.

Sheila learned a lot from her father and his friends. She had many great musical experiences growing up. Unfortunately, musicians usually do not make a lot of money, especially when they are just starting their careers. This meant that the Escovedo family was poor. Sheila and her brothers, Juan José and Peter Michael, and sister, Zina grew up in a rough neighborhood on Oakland's east side.

Sheila remembers how hurt she was when she found out that she could not join the Girl Scouts because she did not have the money to buy the uniform. "It was heartbreaking," she said. Sheila attended three elementary schools: Bella Vista in kindergarten, Garfield Elementary for first and second grades, and Franklin Elementary for third through sixth grades.

"Living in that area, you're forced to be in gangs and involved in things like that," Sheila said. "I ended up having to join a gang in the neighborhood and I had to join a gang in school. I remember I was playing tetherball with my best friend. I went up to my best friend and I hit her as hard as I could in the face. The girls who were always picking on me and beating me up took me aside and said, 'Wow, you're as crazy as us.' They never touched me

Sheila remembers how hurt she was that she could not join the Girl Scouts because she did not have the money to buy a uniform.

again. I had to apologize to my friend. I was lucky she forgave me."

At Montera Junior High, Sheila had to prove herself all over again in seventh and eighth grades. "Everyone has to test you to see how crazy you are, and in order to stop getting beat up you have to go their way or get beat up every day. I got tired of it, so I went their way. I hung around with them, carried knives and things to scare people," she said.

Sheila credits running away from the gangs every day during elementary school for her quickness. "I broke a lot of records in the 50-yard dash, the 220, and the 440 relays," Sheila said. She won many awards and medals and was one of the fastest girls in school.

Even though she was good in track, she was still sad because of all the gangs and prejudice in her neighborhood. "The time I grew up was very racial," Sheila remembered. She grew up in the 1970s, when the United States began busing children, who were mostly Hispanic and Black, from poor neighborhoods into middle-class Anglo schools. Sheila was bused to Montera Junior High School, which was in an area called Oakland Hills. Oakland Hills was the rich part of town, and many people in the area were against this busing. So the children being bused to a new school were met by angry, rude, and scared parents, teachers, and students. "It was very black or white. I was in the middle because I was mixed. So it was either go on one side or the other. I hung out with the Afro-Americans at that time because my mother is Creole and my father is Mexican-American." Creole means being part French and part Black. Sheila is French, Black, and Mexican-American.

A good example of just how hard it was back then can be seen by looking at how it split Sheila's own family. Sheila attended the Montera school with her cousin, who had lighter skin than Sheila's. People paid attention to those little differences, and her cousin chose to hang out with Anglos, while Sheila chose to hang around with Blacks.

"It was strange to be in school with family because we were on two separate sides," Sheila said. "The people I hung around with—I was very dark at the

Sheila was bused to Montera Junior High School. The children being bused were met by angry, rude, and scared parents, teachers, and students.

time—we would purposely pick on anyone lighter than us. Most of the time I didn't like doing what I was doing, but I did it anyway."

Sheila did manage to escape the bad forces of her childhood. What saved her was music. The same instrument her father did not want his daughter to play—the drums—gave her the recognition and purpose she needed as a young girl.

Chapter 3
Playing Percussion

Getting to play the drums and congas was hard to do in the Escovedo house because her father, Pete, did not want Sheila to play. When Pete realized that Sheila wanted to play percussion, he tried to sway her another way. "Only because it's a struggle. It's a constant struggle," Pete said about not wanting Sheila or any of his children to become musicians. "One day you're a star, then one day you're a failure. It's an emotional yo-yo. And [because she was] female, it would be twice as hard for her."

Sheila remembers her father telling her that she would not play percussion. "He told me, 'I don't want you to play

Sheila's father did not want her to play the drums.

percussion. I want you to be something better than that.' He had been struggling as a percussionist since he was fifteen," Sheila said.

He even went so far as to make Sheila play violin. "I knew she had a lot of talent," Pete said. "I wanted her to be a classical musician." So she learned the violin and played for five years. "I was still playing violin up until I was fifteen," Sheila said.

Sheila's father made her play the violin for many years until she convinced him that percussion was for her.

Then she and her mother convinced her father to let her audition for his band Azteca. "Playing percussion with my father that night changed my mind and made me forget violin," Sheila said. She got the job and played percussion for her father that night in San Francisco, at a rally for then-mayor George Moscone, and many nights afterward. "We played to a full house at the Civic Center. We looked at each other in the middle of the show at some point, and we both started crying. It was the most amazing thing that had ever happened to me," she said about playing in front of 3,000 people. "He asked me to do a solo, and I didn't even know what a solo was. He said, 'Just go ahead and play.' I started playing and the people responded. I got chills. I thought, 'If this is what heaven is like, then that is where I want to be.' At the end of the night I told my dad, 'This is what I want to do for the rest of my life.'"

Her father remembers that night as well. "When it actually happened I could not believe her intensity," Pete said. "She had it in her eyes. When we

Her mother convinced her father to let her try out for his band.

looked at each other, it was like we had died and gone to heaven. That was it. I told her she was in the band. People just went crazy over her."

Sheila quit school in eleventh grade at San Leandro High School to tour full-time in the band, with her parents' permission. They agreed to let her go because she wasn't doing very well in school, she took to music naturally, and her work ethic was excellent. Sheila only has one regret: "I regret not having finished school. Now, I realize it's the most important thing a child can do. Learning is very important."

Sheila's one regret in life is that she didn't finish school. Only later did she realize how important school was.

Chapter 4
Life on the Road

Sheila played in her father's band and toured South America. She and her father also played percussion on drummer Billy Cobham's album. He, in turn, produced the two albums Pete and Sheila recorded together, *Solo Two* and *Happy Together*. The albums were released by a record label called Fantasy Records. Through Cobham, Sheila met George Duke, another musician, who was putting a band together for a record and tour. Sheila, then eighteen years old, played and toured with the George Duke Band for several years and recorded four albums with him. She met many people during the tours with Duke, one of whom was the artist then

Sheila and her father recorded two albums together.

known as Prince, in 1978. Prince was the musician who later would give her the confidence to sing and begin a solo career.

During her time with Duke, Sheila's fame spread, and she began recording with many artists like Al Jarreau, Diana Ross, Jeffrey Osborne, and Marvin Gaye. Sheila was working to get a band of her own together when singer Lionel Richie asked her to join his band for an upcoming tour. She did, and

Sheila credits the artist formerly known as Prince with giving her the confidence to sing and begin a solo career of her own.

it proved to be a good idea, because she met up with Prince again in 1983 when he was working on his movie *Purple Rain*. He wanted Sheila to work on some songs and projects with him, which she did.

Prince asked Sheila to sing with him on a record. Sheila said no at first, because she never felt comfortable behind a microphone. She got past her fears as she remembered that she did backup singing with Lionel Richie's band. So she agreed to sing with Prince. Then she found out there were bad words in the song she would be singing, and she didn't like that very much, either. "It was the song 'Erotic City.' There were a lot of bad words in the song and I didn't necessarily have to say them. He said them for me and we did the song and it was a huge hit," Sheila said.

After Sheila and Prince recorded the song "Erotic City," he suggested that she should make her own record. Easier said than done, Sheila thought, but Prince said it wouldn't be hard. He even got her a record deal with Warner Brothers. In 1984 she put out a record

Sheila joined Lionel Ritchie on one of his tours.

titled *Sheila E. in the Glamorous Life*. It only took her a week to record. "With him in the position he was in, I was able to do anything I wanted to do on the record," Sheila said. "We did the record and walked it into the record company. We had the idea of what we wanted to do, the whole concept of how they should sell it. The first disagreement we had with the record company was that they wanted to release 'Belle of St. Mark' as the first single and we wanted to put out 'Glamorous Life.' There was an argument there, but we ended up winning, and it was a hit."

However, it wasn't an overnight hit. Sheila and Prince made sure it would become a winner by working behind the scenes. Sheila worked ten hours every day on publicity for her album before hitting the stage at night to play. It was two-month ordeal. After touring Europe she came to the United States and rehearsed with Prince to play on his *Purple Rain* tour in 1985.

It was this tour that Zina, the youngest of the Escovedo family, remembers vividly because she was in high school at the time.

"What I liked most was when she was on tour with Prince and she'd call me up and ask if I wanted to fly to New York to help her. I loved to be backstage. She would always ask me to help her with stuff. I had to make sure to get her costumes ready and put out her jewelry. I felt so responsible in there taking care of all her clothes," Zina recalled. "All the stars would come backstage constantly. Prince was one of them, and Bette Midler, too. When you're a star and you

Sheila went on tour with Prince.

meet with other stars, you're immediately friends, even if you don't know each other. They would walk backstage, somebody like Wesley Snipes, and they would be real calm and even give each other a kiss on the cheek. Sheila would say hi and act calm until they left the room; then she would jump up and down and say, 'Do you know who that was?' and I know the other stars were saying the same thing about meeting Sheila E."

However, being the sister of a celebrity did have its drawbacks. "Sometimes the public hurt me when they would say things like: 'Why aren't you like your sister? Why aren't you a musician—it's in your blood.' They made me feel like I was beneath my family," Zina said. "It was hard for me to make friends at school. I was so shy. I never knew if people really wanted to be my friend or wanted to use me to get to Sheila. Through the years I started seeing the difference. Life teaches you and I can see through people now."

Life taught Sheila that hard work does pay off, and when she got home from the *Purple Rain* tour she found out

> **Life taught Sheila that hard work does pay off.**

that her album *Sheila E. in the Glamorous Life* had hit the top of the sales charts.

"I think that was the most tired I had ever been in my life. I was totally exhausted," she said.

Her father continues to be amazed by his oldest. "She loves the business. If she's in it she's going to do it right. She's a workaholic and perfectionist," he said about Sheila's work ethic.

Sheila often sings in addition to playing the drums.

Chapter 5
Too Much Work

Sheila was always working and did not take time off to relax.

Sheila's tough work ethic got her into trouble later in her career. Because she was constantly working, there was no time to relax. In 1985 Sheila had a grueling schedule. After the *Purple Rain* tour she starred in her first movie, *Krush Groove*, and released her second record in the fall titled *Sheila E. in Romance 1600*. She continued to work for others and for herself in 1986. She toured with Lionel Richie in the United States and started work on her third album, titled *Sheila E*. Instead of touring behind that album, she decided to work with Prince again and played drums for his *Sign O' the Times* tour.

The frantic pace caught up with Sheila in 1990. While she was recording her fourth solo record, her body told her it was time to take a break.

"Near the end of recording my record, because I had never stopped, my body just shut down. My back went out. I was paralyzed for two weeks. I couldn't walk. We flew doctors into Minneapolis [Minnesota], where I was living, to try to help me get back on my feet. It took a couple of months for me to recover. I was also getting acupuncture on my back to help it heal, but I think they punctured my lung." Acupuncture is an old Chinese practice of picking someone with thin needles to relieve pain.

When Sheila left the acupuncturist's office, her left hand felt numb. But she thought nothing of it and went back to the studio to finish her record. She worked for three days until she could no longer stand the pain and went into the hospital, where a doctor told her that eighty percent of her lung had collapsed. "I couldn't breathe, but I thought I was just exhausted. I got really sick. It was at this time I thought I had

The frantic pace caught up with her in 1990. Her back went out and she was paralyzed for two weeks.

to change my life," she said. "I realized it is important to sleep, take a break, and sit down and eat a regular meal. I wasn't doing drugs or drinking or anything like that, it was just that I really loved what I did. It was my life."

This brought on a bigger change in Sheila's life than she ever imagined. Her sickness, she said, "brought me closer to God." No longer part of large touring bands, Sheila took it easy and played in several bands of her own. She recorded a special concert with her father and the man she calls her uncle, musician Tito Puente. The show was released on a CD titled *Latina Familia*.

Her fourth album, *Sex Cymbal*, was released in 1991. During this time, Sheila did a lot of session work with a number of artists. Session work means she played on other people's albums. She also performed at the Academy Awards in 1993 with Plácido Domingo and at the Grammy Awards show with Gloria Estefan. In 1994 she introduced her soul, Latin, jazz, funk, fusion, and gospel band called E-Train. She toured with her band and did more session work, and continued to perform at several shows.

In 1993, Sheila performed at the Academy Awards with Plácido Domingo.

Chapter 6
A New Life

It was during her healing time that she heard from Magic Johnson, the former Los Angeles Lakers basketball player. She said she met him during her tours with the artist formerly known as Prince. "He would come and see the band like many other huge stars," Sheila said. "That's where I first met him."

In 1997 Johnson called Sheila when she was going to tour in Japan. "He called me late at night and said, 'Look I've been trying to find you and want to talk to you about something.'"

But because she was going out on tour the next day for two and a half months, she asked him to tell her what the meetings were going to be about. At

In 1997, Magic Johnson asked Sheila to lead the band for his new TV show.

first he hesitated, then he said he was hosting a talk show and he wanted Sheila to be his musical director. She was very interested and became the first female band director on a late night television talk show, *The Magic Hour*. "It was an honor and a privilege to be the first woman musical director on late night television," she said. The show lasted on the air for several months, exposing Sheila to a whole new audience.

"As I broke into the studio scene, I realized how tough it was going to be, because the moment I walked into a studio, most of the male drummers had a weird attitude toward me. I didn't consider the drums [to be] a male instrument. It was very normal to me. It had always been a part of my life. It was very strange to hear other drummers saying things to discourage me," Sheila said in *Latin Style* magazine. "I would go to my dad and share my feelings. He explained to me about the business and that with it comes jealousy."

"Women were not allowed to play drums," Pete said. "She went through a lot to prove she is a musician. She's a

> **Sheila has been determined to succeed in a male-dominated field.**

great one, really. You can sit her down in a room with a hundred instruments and she'll go and pick up any instrument and she could play it in ten minutes. She's one of the very blessed and fortunate."

She used her blessings wisely and was determined to succeed in a male-dominated profession. And she has, producing four albums throughout her career, and working steadily with big-name musicians. In 1999, she opened her own recording studio.

Sheila E. proved her strength the day she convinced her father that she was good enough to play with professional musicians. She didn't let inexperience stop her and she won't let anything get in her way. It's a lesson everyone should take to heart.

Robin Williams (left), Andre Agassi and Sheila E. sing along during the finale of the Grand Slam at the MGM Grand Garden on September 26, 1998 in Las Vegas, Nevada.

Chronology

1957　Born December 12, in Oakland, California; mother: Juanita Gardere; father: Latin jazz musician, Pete Escovedo
1972　At age 15, played in her father's band, Azteca
1975　At age 18, played and toured with the George Duke band
1978　first met the artist then known as Prince
1984　records album *Sheila E. in the Glamorous Life*
1985　*Purple Rain* tour with Prince; starred in first movie, *Krush Groove*; released second album *Sheila E. in Romance 1600*
1986　toured with Lionel Richie; played drums for Prince in *Sign O' the Times* tour
1987　released third album, *Sheila E.*
1989　recorded special concert with her father and Tito Puente
1991　released album *Sex Cymbal*
1994　introduces band E-Train
1997　becomes first female band director on late night TV for *The Magic Hour*
1999　starts her own recording studio

Index